# Polygamy as Heritage

## Debunking the Neo-colonial Critique in African Societies

JOHN EGYAWAN

# DEDICATION

This work is dedicated to the ancestors of African culture and heritage, whose wisdom, resilience, and spirit have woven the rich tapestry of our continent. It is through their trials and triumphs that we understand the depth of our roots and the breadth of our potential.

In the same breath, this dedication extends to the Pan-Africanist movement, a beacon of hope and solidarity in the ongoing journey to reclaim Africa from the grips of neocolonialism. The movement's enduring commitment to unity, sovereignty, and cultural pride serves as a guiding light for future generations seeking to honor the legacy of our ancestors while forging a path toward a continent defined by its autonomy, dignity, and prosperity.

May this work contribute to the ongoing dialogue about our diverse cultures and family structures, serving as a reminder of the strength found in our heritage and the power of collective action in the face of modern challenges.

To the ancestors and to the Pan-Africanist movement, this is for you—a testament to the enduring spirit of Africa and its people.

# CONTENTS

# FORWARD

In an era where the tapestry of human culture and identity is increasingly under the scrutiny of globalization and modernity, "Polygamy as Heritage: Debunking the Neo-colonial Critique in African Societies" emerges as a crucial discourse that challenges prevailing narratives and offers a profound reexamination of African societal norms, particularly in relation to polygamy. Authored by John Egyawan, also revered as Bishop John, this work stands as a beacon of understanding, offering both a scholarly analysis and a heartfelt plea for the acknowledgment and respect of African cultural practices.

Bishop John's exploration into the multifaceted world of polygamy in African societies is not merely an academic endeavor; it is a journey into the heart of Africa itself. It is a quest to unveil the truths that lie within centuries-old traditions, shedding light on the intricate balance of social, economic, and spiritual forces that have shaped African family structures. This book delves into the historical context of polygamy, tracing its roots back to the cradle of humanity, through the tumultuous era of colonialism, and into the present day, where African societies grapple with the legacy of colonial imposition and the challenges of modernity.

The author navigates this complex terrain with the grace and wisdom of a seasoned scholar and the compassion of a spiritual leader. He challenges the reader to see beyond the simplistic dichotomies of right and wrong, tradition and modernity, African and Western. Instead, Bishop John invites us into a dialogue—a conversation that respects the diversity of human experience and acknowledges the validity of multiple forms of family and community.

What makes this work particularly poignant is its call to action. It is not content with merely presenting an analysis; it urges African societies and indeed, the global community, to embrace a more inclusive understanding of family structures. It advocates for a world where polygamy is recognized not as a relic of the past but as a living, breathing aspect of African culture that continues to have relevance and value.

As we stand at the crossroads of history, facing the dual challenges of preserving cultural identity while navigating the waters of global change, "Polygamy as Heritage" offers a compass. It reminds us that the path to understanding and acceptance is paved with respect, dialogue, and an unwavering commitment to the dignity of all peoples.

This forward does not merely introduce a book; it heralds a movement towards a deeper appreciation of Africa's rich cultural heritage and its enduring significance in our shared human story. It is with great honor and anticipation that I invite you to journey through these pages, guided by the insightful and compassionate hand of Bishop John.

# 1 CHAPTER ONE

## Historical and Cultural Context of Polygamy in Africa

## Introduction to the Chapter

Polygamy, the practice of having more than one spouse at a time, has been a significant aspect of many African cultures for centuries. Far from being a mere marital preference, polygamy in African societies has historically been a complex institution, interwoven with various social, economic, and political fabrics. This chapter aims to explore the historical roots of polygamy in Africa, understanding how it has been integrated and manifested in different cultures across the continent.

## The Origins and Evolution of Polygamy in African Societies

To comprehend the role of polygamy in African history, one must look back to the ancient civilizations that dotted the continent. From the great kingdoms of West Africa to the diverse tribes of the East and South, polygamy was prevalent in various forms. In many cases, it was a symbol of wealth and social status; the ability to support multiple wives and children was often indicative of a man's wealth and his ability to provide.

## Social Functions and Integration

Polygamy played several crucial social functions. In agrarian societies, a larger family meant more hands to work the land, which was essential for survival and prosperity. In pastoral communities, numerous family members ensured the efficient management of livestock. Beyond economic benefits, polygamy also served to strengthen alliances and relationships between different families and clans, thus fostering community cohesion and stability.

## Roles and Responsibilities within Polygamous Families

Within the polygamous family structure, each member had distinct roles and responsibilities, which were often governed by well-defined cultural norms. The senior wife usually held a position of respect and authority, playing a pivotal role in household management and the upbringing of children. Younger wives were integrated into the family system, each contributing to the household's economic and social welfare. Children from these unions were raised in a communal setting, often forming strong bonds with their siblings and extended family members.

## Cultural Variations Across the Continent

It is crucial to recognize the diversity in the practice of polygamy across different African cultures. For instance, in some societies, polygamy was matrilineal, where lineage and inheritance were traced through the mother. In others, it was patrilineal, with emphasis on the father's lineage. These variations were not mere marital arrangements but were deeply rooted in the cosmologies and worldviews of the respective cultures.

## Polygamy and its Relation to African Religions and Beliefs

Religion and traditional beliefs also played a significant role in the practice of polygamy. African traditional religions, with their emphasis on ancestor worship and the importance of progeny, often viewed polygamy favorably. The continuity of the family line and the appeasement of ancestors were crucial aspects of these religions, and polygamy was seen as a means to fulfill these objectives.

## Conclusion

In conclusion, the historical and cultural context of polygamy in Africa reveals its deep-rooted significance in the continent's social and cultural tapestry. Far from being a simplistic or monolithic practice, it is a complex institution that has evolved over centuries, shaped by economic needs, social structures, and religious beliefs. Understanding this context is essential in appreciating the role of polygamy in African societies, beyond the simplistic critiques often leveled against it from external perspectives.

# 2 CHAPTER TWO

## Impact of European Colonialism and Missionaries on African Societal Norms

## Introduction to the Chapter

The advent of European colonialism and missionary efforts in Africa marked a profound shift in the continent's societal fabric, particularly in the realm of family structures and marital practices. This chapter delves into the profound impact of these external influences, with a focus on how the introduction of Christian monogamy served as a tool for cultural assimilation and a means to reshape African societies in line with European values.

## The Onset of European Influence in Africa

The arrival of European colonizers and missionaries in Africa brought with it not only political and economic changes but also a wave of cultural transformations. European powers, driven by a blend of imperial ambition and religious zeal, embarked on a mission to 'civilize' the African populace, which often entailed imposing their own values and beliefs.

## Christian Monogamy as a Cultural Imposition

Central to this cultural imposition was the promotion of Christian monogamy. For the European missionaries, polygamy was seen as a barbaric and pagan practice that needed to be eradicated. The Christian model of a nuclear family, consisting of one man, one woman, and their children, was presented as the civilized and moral alternative. This perspective was not merely a religious stance but a reflection of the broader European worldview at the time.

## Strategies of Cultural Assimilation

The strategies employed to enforce this shift were multifaceted. Missionary schools taught the virtues of monogamy and the Christian family model, while colonial laws increasingly criminalized and marginalized polygamous unions. Converts to Christianity were often required to abandon polygamy and adopt monogamous marriages as a testament to their faith and civilization.

## The Impact on African Societies

This imposition of monogamy had far-reaching impacts on African societies. It disrupted traditional family structures, often causing social and familial discord. The undermining of polygamous practices also had broader implications, affecting social networks, inheritance patterns, and community dynamics. The shift towards monogamy was not a seamless transition but a source of significant tension and conflict within communities.

## Resistance and Adaptation

Despite these pressures, many African societies showed resilience and adaptability. Some integrated aspects of Christian teachings while maintaining polygamous practices, albeit in modified forms. Others resisted outright, viewing the preservation of their traditional marital practices as an act of cultural and spiritual defiance against colonial rule.

## Conclusion

The impact of European colonialism and missionary efforts on African societal norms, particularly in the context of marriage and family structures, is a testament to the complex interplay between external influences and indigenous cultures. The introduction of Christian monogamy, far from being a benign cultural exchange, was a deliberate strategy of cultural assimilation, aimed at reshaping African societies to conform to European ideals. Understanding this historical context is crucial in appreciating the ongoing debates and dynamics surrounding family structures in contemporary African societies.

# 3 CHAPTER THREE

## Monogamy as a Neo-colonial Tool

## Introduction to the Chapter

While the imposition of monogamy in African societies during the colonial era was often framed as a moral and cultural imperative by European powers, this chapter argues that it was also a strategic tool for neo-colonial control. The promotion of monogamy served not just to impose European cultural values but also to influence and manage population growth and familial structures in a way that benefitted colonial objectives.

## The Strategic Motives Behind Promoting Monogamy

At the heart of the colonial agenda was the desire to exert control over the African populace. By promoting monogamy, colonial powers aimed to disrupt traditional social structures and familial bonds, which were seen as a source of strength and resilience for African communities. By weakening these structures, colonial authorities hoped to create a more malleable and controllable society.

## Historical Evidence and Statements

This perspective is supported by various historical documents and statements from the colonial era. For instance, colonial administrators often expressed concerns about the difficulty of controlling large polygamous families and the challenge they posed to the establishment of colonial rule. Furthermore, some colonial policies explicitly encouraged monogamous marriages, often tying them to benefits such as access to education, land, and employment in the colonial administration.

## Population Control and Economic Objectives

Another aspect of this strategy was the control of population growth. By promoting monogamy and reducing family sizes, colonial powers aimed to manage the demographic development of African societies. This was seen as crucial not only for easier governance but also for economic reasons. Smaller family units required fewer resources and were less likely to unite in large-scale resistance against colonial rule.

## The Long-Term Impact on African Societies

The long-term impact of this shift towards monogamy was profound. It altered not only family structures but also the social and economic dynamics of African societies. In many cases, it led to a fragmentation of communities and a weakening of traditional support systems, effects that are still felt in various forms today.

## Conclusion

The promotion of monogamy in African societies by European colonialists was a complex and multifaceted strategy. It went beyond cultural imperialism, serving as a tool for population control, social management, and economic manipulation. This chapter underscores the importance of viewing the shift from polygamy to monogamy in Africa not just as a cultural change, but as part of a broader neo-colonial agenda with lasting implications.

# 4 CHAPTER FOUR

## Contemporary Perspectives and Misconceptions of Polygamy

## Introduction to the Chapter

In the modern era, the practice of polygamy continues to evoke a wide range of reactions and perspectives both within African societies and globally. This chapter aims to dissect contemporary views on polygamy, addressing common misconceptions and contrasting them with the realities of polygamous practices as they exist in various African contexts today.

## Global Perceptions of Polygamy

Globally, polygamy often faces criticism and is frequently misunderstood. In many Western societies, where monogamy is the predominant marital norm, polygamy is often viewed through a lens of moral judgment and is associated with negative stereotypes such as gender oppression, sexual promiscuity, and social backwardness. These perceptions are influenced by a combination of cultural biases, media portrayals, and a lack of understanding of the complexities and variations within polygamous practices.

## Contemporary African Perspectives

Within Africa, the perspective on polygamy is more nuanced. While the practice continues in many communities, its prevalence and social acceptance vary widely across different regions and cultures. In some areas, polygamy remains a respected and integral part of the social fabric, while in others, it has diminished due to urbanization, economic changes, and the influence of Western values. Additionally, the modern African perspective is often a blend of traditional views and contemporary realities, reflecting the dynamic nature of African societies.

## Addressing Common Misconceptions

One major misconception about polygamy is that it inherently devalues women and is synonymous with female subjugation.

However, in many African societies practicing polygamy, women play significant and respected roles, both within the family and the broader community. The structure and dynamics of polygamous households are diverse, and in some cases, they provide women with unique forms of social and economic support.

Another misconception is the idea that polygamy is primarily driven by male sexual desires. In reality, the motivations for polygamy are varied and often include economic considerations, social status, the desire for children, and the maintenance of family lineage.

## The Realities of Polygamous Practices

The realities of polygamous practices in African societies are complex and cannot be painted with a broad brush. While there are undoubtedly challenges and issues associated with polygamy, including potential family conflicts and economic strain, these are not universally experienced and depend greatly on the specific cultural and societal context.

## Conclusion

Understanding the contemporary perspectives and misconceptions about polygamy requires a nuanced and context-sensitive approach. It is essential to move beyond stereotypes and generalized views to appreciate the varied experiences and realities of polygamous practices in African societies. This chapter highlights the importance of engaging with polygamy as a dynamic and multifaceted institution, one that continues to evolve in response to changing social, economic, and cultural forces.

# 5 CHAPTER FIVE

## Polygamy and Women's Rights

## Introduction to the Chapter

The intersection of polygamy and women's rights is a subject of significant debate and importance. This chapter explores the complex relationship between polygamous practices and the rights and empowerment of women within these marital structures, addressing both the challenges and potential avenues for ensuring respect and empowerment.

## Challenges Faced by Women in Polygamous Marriages

One of the primary concerns in polygamous marriages is the potential for inequalities and injustices faced by women. Issues such as unequal treatment among wives, financial dependency, limited decision-making power, and the risk of marginalization are real challenges that need acknowledgment and address. In some cases, women in polygamous marriages may also face social stigma and legal challenges, particularly in regions where polygamy is not legally recognized.

## Cultural Context and Women's Empowerment

It is crucial to understand the cultural context in which polygamous marriages occur. In many African societies, women in polygamous families play significant roles and have substantial influence in family and community matters. These roles can provide a platform for empowerment and respect. Additionally, the communal and supportive nature of extended polygamous families can offer women a network of assistance and solidarity that is often overlooked in Western critiques.

## Legal and Societal Frameworks Supporting Women's Rights

Addressing women's rights in polygamous marriages requires robust legal and societal frameworks. This involves ensuring that women's rights are protected within marriage, including rights to property, inheritance, and decision-making. Legal recognition of polygamous marriages in some African countries is a step toward this, as it provides a framework for protecting the rights and interests of all parties involved.

## Empowering Women Within Polygamous Structures

Empowerment within polygamous marriages can take various forms. Education and economic independence are crucial. Ensuring that women have access to education and the opportunity to engage in economic activities empowers them to make informed decisions and contributes to their financial independence. Encouraging and supporting the active participation of women in family decision-making processes also plays a critical role.

## The Role of Community and Cultural Leaders

Community and cultural leaders have a significant role in shaping attitudes and practices within polygamous marriages. Their support for the rights and empowerment of women can lead to positive changes. Initiatives led by these leaders to educate and raise awareness about women's rights and the importance of equitable and respectful treatment within polygamous families can have a substantial impact.

## Conclusion

Polygamy and women's rights is a multifaceted issue that requires a balanced and context-sensitive approach. While acknowledging the challenges, it is essential to recognize and support the structures within polygamous practices that can empower and respect women. Efforts to enhance women's rights in polygamous marriages must be grounded in the cultural, social, and legal realities of the societies in which they occur.

19

# 6 CHAPTER SIX

## The Case for Polygamy as a Valid Family Structure

## Introduction to the Chapter

Polygamy, often sidelined in modern discourse on family structures, deserves a reevaluation for its potential benefits and legitimacy as a form of family organization. This chapter presents a case for recognizing polygamy as a valid and viable family structure, highlighting its contributions to social stability, economic support systems, and cultural continuity.

## Polygamy and Social Stability

One of the key arguments in favor of polygamy is its role in promoting social stability. In many traditional African societies, polygamous marriages contribute to the formation of extensive familial networks, creating strong bonds and alliances among different families and communities. These extended networks provide a support system that can contribute to social cohesion and stability. Additionally, in societies where there is a gender imbalance, polygamy can provide a solution by ensuring that more individuals have the opportunity to marry and have families.

## Economic Benefits of Polygamous Structures

Polygamy can also offer substantial economic benefits. In agrarian and pastoral societies, larger family units can manage land and livestock more effectively. In modern contexts, these extended families can pool resources to support each other, particularly in times of economic hardship. This communal approach to economics can provide a safety net for family members, reducing the impact of poverty and financial instability.

## Cultural Continuity and Polygamy

Cultural continuity is another significant aspect of polygamy. For many African communities, polygamous marriages are not just about personal or economic interests; they are a way of preserving cultural heritage and traditions. Through polygamy, cultural values and practices are passed down through generations, ensuring the continuity of these traditions. Polygamy also plays a role in lineage and inheritance practices, which are crucial aspects of many African cultures.

## Polygamy in the Context of Modern Societies

In the context of modern societies, polygamy can still offer a viable alternative family structure. It challenges the conventional nuclear family model and provides a framework for a more communal and cooperative form of family life. In a world where the definitions of family and marriage are constantly evolving, polygamy offers a perspective that values extended familial networks and communal living.

## Addressing Challenges and Misconceptions

While advocating for polygamy as a valid family structure, it is essential to address the challenges and work towards models of polygamous marriages that are equitable and respectful of all members. Education and legal frameworks play a crucial role in ensuring that polygamous marriages are conducted in a manner that upholds the rights and dignity of all involved.

## Conclusion

The case for polygamy as a legitimate form of family structure is grounded in its potential for social stability, economic benefits, and cultural continuity. Recognizing polygamy as a valid option in the spectrum of family structures allows for a more inclusive understanding of family and marriage, one that respects the diversity of cultural practices and values.

# 7 CHAPTER SEVEN

## Christian Views on Polygamy: A Balanced Perspective

## Introduction to the Chapter

The Christian perspective on polygamy is a subject of considerable debate and interpretation, with viewpoints varying significantly across different denominations and cultural contexts. This chapter aims to present a balanced view of the Christian stance on polygamy, examining both historical and contemporary perspectives, and exploring the scriptural references that have informed these views.

## Polygamy in the Old Testament

The practice of polygamy is indeed documented in the Old Testament, where several prominent figures, including Abraham, Jacob, David, and Solomon, had multiple wives. These instances are presented without explicit condemnation, suggesting a cultural acceptance of polygamy in the historical context of these narratives. For instance, 2 Samuel 12:8, where God, speaking through the prophet Nathan, says to David, "I gave your master's house to you, and your master's wives into your arms," can be interpreted as a tacit acknowledgment of polygamous practices.

## The New Testament and Monogamy

In the New Testament, the focus shifts more towards monogamous unions, particularly in the context of church leadership. Verses such as 1 Timothy 3:2 and Titus 1:6, which state that a bishop or deacon should be the husband of but one wife, are often cited in support of monogamy. However, these references are specific to church leadership and are not universally prescribed as a mandate for all Christians.

## Theological Arguments for and Against Polygamy

From a theological standpoint, arguments against polygamy often point to Jesus' teachings on marriage, particularly in Matthew 19:4-6, where He refers to the Genesis account of creation, emphasizing the union of one man and one woman. Proponents of polygamy, however, argue that this interpretation does not explicitly prohibit polygamy but rather sets a precedent for the ideal marriage.

## Contemporary Christian Perspectives

In contemporary Christian discourse, attitudes towards polygamy vary widely. Some denominations maintain a strict stance against it, viewing monogamy as the ideal Christian marriage model. Others adopt a more contextual approach, especially in regions where polygamy is culturally prevalent and has been integrated with Christian practices.

## Conclusion

The Christian views on polygamy present a complex tapestry of historical, cultural, and theological perspectives. While the Old Testament provides examples of polygamous relationships among key figures, the New Testament shifts the focus towards monogamy, especially in the context of church leadership. Contemporary interpretations continue to vary, reflecting the diverse contexts in which Christianity is practiced. Ultimately, the Christian perspective on polygamy is multifaceted and cannot be reduced to a single, definitive stance.

# 8 CHAPTER EIGHT

## Author's View: Embracing Polygamy in African Christianity

As the author of this exploration into the complexities of polygamy within African societies and its intersection with Christian beliefs, I hold a firm stance on the issue of polygamy in the Christian context, particularly in Africa. It is my belief that the outright prohibition of polygamists from participating in Christian communion and other religious activities is a misstep, grounded more in man-made doctrines than in the Gospel's message of grace and the new covenant.

## The Gospel of Grace and Polygamous Christians

The Gospel of grace, as presented in the New Testament, is an invitation to all, irrespective of their marital practices. To deny polygamists the right to partake in communion or other Christian ordinances is to impose human restrictions on a Gospel that is inherently about divine acceptance and love. There is a notable absence in the scriptures of any directive that demands polygamists to divorce their additional spouses, save for the first. Those advocating for such actions are, in my view, overstepping their bounds, placing human judgment above divine wisdom.

## Cultural Ostracization and the African Church

The tendency of African Christians to ostracize African cultures and traditions in favor of European ones is a concerning trend that needs addressing. The assumption of European family structures' superiority over African ones lacks empirical evidence and, more importantly, disregards the rich diversity and validity of African familial arrangements. It is crucial to recognize that no single cultural model of family structure is universally superior.

## Neocolonialism and the African Church

The African Church's role in perpetuating neocolonialism is a topic that requires introspection and critique. Just as some African churches have adopted European attire as the standard for sacred wear, similarly, there has been a tendency to favor Western musical instruments over traditional African ones. This practice subtly undermines African culture, promoting a Eurocentric worldview that is often at odds with African heritage. The church, in many ways, has been instrumental in the neocolonial endeavor, aiding in the detachment of Africans from their cultural roots, not just in family structures but also in broader cultural and political spheres.

## Conclusion and Call for Change

In conclusion, it is imperative for the African Church to reevaluate its stance on polygamy and its broader approach to African culture and traditions. A more inclusive and culturally sensitive approach, one that respects the diverse family structures and cultural practices in Africa, is essential. The church should lead in bridging cultural gaps, not widening them, and in doing so, play a role in healing the scars of colonialism and neocolonialism. Only through such a transformation can the church truly embody the inclusive and accepting spirit of the Gospel.

# ACKNOWLEDGEMENTS

As the author of this comprehensive exploration into the multifaceted world of polygamy within African societies and its intersection with Christian beliefs, I extend my deepest gratitude to a number of individuals and institutions whose contributions have been invaluable.

Firstly, I wish to express my heartfelt thanks to the various African communities and families who generously shared their insights and experiences. Their openness and willingness to discuss a subject that is often surrounded by misconceptions and sensitivities have been the backbone of this work. Their stories and perspectives have provided a depth of understanding that has been crucial in shaping this narrative.

Special appreciation is extended to the scholars and academics whose works have been instrumental in the research for this article. Their rigorous analyses and dedicated research into African societal norms, the impacts of colonialism, and the integration of traditional practices within Christian contexts have been foundational to this study. I am particularly indebted to those who have focused their careers on exploring the complex dynamics of family structures and women's roles within polygamous societies.

I am also grateful to the various theologians and religious leaders who provided their insights into the Christian views on polygamy. Their diverse perspectives have been essential in presenting a balanced and nuanced exploration of this topic within the context of Christian doctrine and practice.

My appreciation also goes out to the reviewers and editors who have painstakingly gone through drafts of this work, providing critical feedback and suggestions that have greatly enhanced the quality and clarity of the final product.

Lastly, I would like to acknowledge my family and friends for their unwavering support and encouragement throughout the writing process. Their belief in the importance of this work has been a constant source of motivation.

This work is a tribute to the rich tapestry of African cultures and the enduring spirit of its people. It is my hope that this article contributes to a greater understanding and appreciation of the diverse family structures that exist not only in Africa but across the world, and fosters a more inclusive and respectful discourse on cultural practices.

## John Egyawan, AKA Bishop John

John Egyawan, widely recognized as Bishop John, is a beacon of hope and transformation whose life work seamlessly weaves together the spiritual, social, and entrepreneurial. His holistic approach to ministry underscores a profound commitment to not just preach the Gospel but to actualize its teachings in every facet of human life—be it through spiritual guidance, social justice advocacy, or economic empowerment.

Raised in a community where solidarity and resilience were daily lived experiences in the suburb of Buea - Ambazonia, John's early encounters with both hardship and communal support shaped his understanding of ministry. It is not just about tending to the soul but equally about addressing the tangible needs of the body and the mind. This conviction has propelled him to integrate practical support and development initiatives alongside spiritual mentorship, making his ministry a robust platform for holistic human flourishing.

Bishop John's entrepreneurial spirit is another testament to his holistic ministry. Recognizing the pivotal role of economic independence in societal wellbeing, he has ventured into various entrepreneurial efforts aimed at creating sustainable development opportunities. Through these endeavors, John seeks to model and inspire a form of Christian entrepreneurship that is ethical, empowering, and in service of the wider community.

The title "Bishop" bestowed upon John Egyawan is a mark of respect and recognition, not of ecclesiastical ascent but of his significant involvement in the Ambazonia struggle. It signifies acknowledgment from within the movement for his unwavering dedication to the cause, his leadership in advocating for reconciliation, peace and justice, and his role in providing spiritual and moral guidance during turbulent times. This title is emblematic of the grassroots respect and authority he holds, a direct consequence of his deep commitment to the wellbeing and liberation of his people.

In "In Their Footsteps: The Christian Mandate for Social Justice," Bishop John invites readers into a reflective journey that marries the depth of Christian doctrine with the urgency of contemporary social action. His writing not only echoes his broad understanding of Scripture and social issues but also showcases his entrepreneurial mindset, presenting a compelling vision for a world where faith actively contributes to societal transformation and economic justice.

Through his multifaceted ministry, entrepreneurial ventures, and the symbolic mantle of Bishop John, he embodies a pathway of service that is deeply rooted in faith and expansively engaged with the world. His life and work challenge us to envision and enact a Christianity that is as concerned with the spiritual as it is with the social and economic dimensions of human life, guiding us toward a future where justice, peace, and prosperity are accessible to all.

**Contact the Author for comments or inquiries.**

**Website: Bishopjohn.com**
**Email: Bishopjohn@gmail.com**
**WhatsApp: +234 808 881-5062**

# REFERENCES

## Scriptures

1. **Old Testament References to Polygamy:**
   - Abraham: Genesis 16:1-4, Genesis 25:1-6
   - Jacob: Genesis 29:16-30
   - David: 2 Samuel 3:2-5, 2 Samuel 5:13-16
   - Solomon: 1 Kings 11:1-3
2. **New Testament References:**
   - Monogamy in Church Leadership: 1 Timothy 3:2, Titus 1:6
   - Jesus' Teaching on Marriage: Matthew 19:4-6

## Historical and Cultural Sources

1. **African Traditional Practices and Polygamy:**
   - Amadiume, Ifi. "Male Daughters, Female Husbands: Gender and Sex in an African Society." Zed Books Ltd, 1987.
   - Mbiti, John S. "African Religions and Philosophy." Heinemann, 1969.
2. **Impact of European Colonialism:**
   - Rodney, Walter. "How Europe Underdeveloped Africa." Bogle-L'Ouverture Publications, 1972.
   - Achebe, Chinua. "Things Fall Apart." Heinemann, 1958 (for a literary perspective).
3. **Contemporary Perspectives on Polygamy:**
   - Nzegwu, Nkiru. "Family Matters: Feminist Concepts in African Philosophy of Culture." SUNY Press, 2006.

- Falola, Toyin and Njoku, Raphael Chijioke. "Warfare and Culture in World History." New York University Press, 2011.

4. **Polygamy and Women's Rights:**
   - Nnaemeka, Obioma. "The Politics of (M)Othering: Womanhood, Identity and Resistance in African Literature." Routledge, 1997.
   - Tamale, Sylvia. "African Feminism: How Should We Change?" Development, 2006.

5. **Christian Views on Polygamy:**
   - Hillman, Eugene. "Polygamy Reconsidered: African Plural Marriage and the Christian Churches." Orbis Books, 1975.
   - Kunhiyop, Samuel Waje. "African Christian Ethics." Zondervan, 2008.

6. **Neocolonialism and the Church:**
   - Fanon, Frantz. "The Wretched of the Earth." Grove Press, 1961.
   - Berman, Bruce J. "Control and Crisis in Colonial Kenya: The Dialectic of Domination." James Currey Publishers, 1990.

## Online Sources

- **African Studies Journals and Online Publications:** For updated scholarly articles and contemporary discussions.
- **Encyclopedia Britannica and JSTOR:** For historical and cultural overviews.